SPORTS SUPERSTARS

CANDACE PARKER

BY INDIA JAMES

BELLWETHER MEDIA · MINNEAPOLIS, MN

Torque brims with excitement perfect for thrill-seekers of all kinds. Discover daring survival skills, explore uncharted worlds, and marvel at mighty engines and extreme sports. In *Torque* books, anything can happen. Are you ready?

This edition first published in 2025 by Bellwether Media, Inc.

Library of Congress Cataloging-in-Publication Data

LC record for Candace Parker available at: https://lccn.loc.gov/2024047006

Editor: Kieran Downs   Designer: Gabriel Hilger

Printed in the United States of America, North Mankato, MN.

TABLE OF

CONTENTS

A BIG BASKET

It is Game 3 of the 2017 **semifinals** of the **Women's National Basketball Association** (WNBA). The Sparks are tied with the Mercury. Time is running out.

Candace Parker of the Sparks drives the ball towards the net. She runs past Mercury players. With 2.9 seconds left, she scores! The Sparks are headed to the WNBA **Finals**!

EquiTrust
3

WHO IS CANDACE PARKER?

Candace Parker is a former WNBA player. She usually played **forward** and **center**. She is known for her **slam dunks**.

CANDACE PARKER

BIRTHDAY	April 19, 1986
HOMETOWN	Naperville, Illinois
POSITION	forward, center
HEIGHT	6 feet 4 inches
DRAFTED	Los Angeles Sparks in the 1st round (1st overall) of the 2008 WNBA Draft

Parker has won **championships** in the WNBA. She has also won **Olympic** gold medals. Today, Parker uses her knowledge of basketball as a **game analyst** for basketball on television.

GETTING THE BALL

Parker grew up in a family that loved sports. Her father was her coach. Parker led her team to two state championships while she was in high school.

PARKER AND HER FATHER

NAPERVILLE CENTRAL HIGH SCHOOL

BASKETBALL FAMILY

PARKER'S OLDER BROTHER, ANTHONY, ALSO PLAYED PROFESSIONAL BASKETBALL. HE PLAYED IN THE NBA.

She was the first female player to slam dunk in a game in Illinois. Parker was also the first female winner of the slam dunk contest at the McDonald's All American Game.

Parker planned to play college basketball at the University of Tennessee. But she hurt her knee before college. Her coach, Pat Summitt, helped her recover.

Parker first played for Tennessee in 2005. In 2007 and 2008, she led Tennessee to championships. She was named the **Most Valuable Player** (MVP) both times.

HIGH SCORE

PARKER SCORED 2,137 POINTS DURING HER THREE YEARS PLAYING AT THE UNIVERSITY OF TENNESSEE.

FAVORITES

SPORT OTHER THAN BASKETBALL

soccer

SNACK

almonds

DRINK

gingerbread latte

SUBJECT

history

2008 NCAA WOMEN'S FINAL FOUR CHAMPIONSHIP

A WINNING PLAYER

In 2008, the Los Angeles Sparks **drafted** Parker. She also played for Team USA at the Beijing Summer Olympics. She helped the team win a gold medal.

Parker played well for the Sparks. She was named the WNBA **Rookie** of the Year in 2008. She was also named the WNBA MVP.

2008 BEIJING SUMMER OLYMPICS

2012 LONDON SUMMER OLYMPICS

Parker was out for a lot of her first few seasons. In 2011, she was named to her first **All-Star Game**. But she was hurt. She could not play. In 2012, Parker helped Team USA win another Olympic gold medal!

In 2013, Parker won her second WNBA MVP. She was also able to play in her first All-Star Game.

CANDACE PARKER MAP

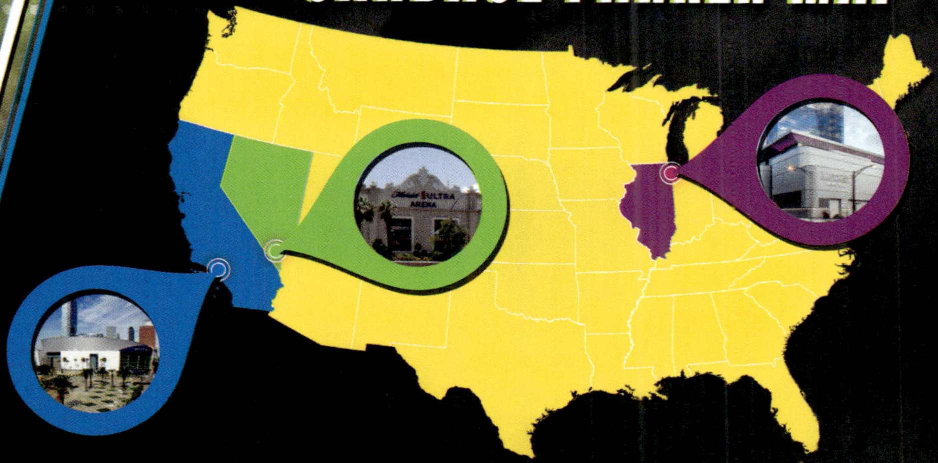

- Los Angeles Sparks, Los Angeles, California 2008 to 2020
- Chicago Sky, Chicago, Illinois 2021 to 2022
- Las Vegas Aces, Las Vegas, Nevada 2023

MORE POINTS

IN 2010, PARKER ONLY PLAYED IN 10 GAMES. BUT SHE AVERAGED MORE THAN 20 POINTS PER GAME!

Parker was out again for much of 2015. But in 2016, she helped the Sparks win the WNBA Finals. Parker was named the Finals MVP. In 2017, she helped the Sparks go back to the Finals. But they lost.

Parker played well in 2018. But she was hurt again in 2019. In 2020, Parker was named the WNBA **Defensive** Player of the Year.

2016 WNBA FINALS

Travels

PARKER HAS PLAYED FOR BASKETBALL TEAMS IN RUSSIA, CHINA, AND TURKEY DURING THE WNBA OFFSEASON.

TROPHY SHELF

3-time WNBA champion

2-time WNBA MVP

2-time Olympic gold medalist

WNBA Rookie of the Year

7-time WNBA All-Star

In 2021, Parker signed with the Chicago Sky. She helped the team win the Finals that year. In 2022, she led the team to their best-ever regular season. But they did not win the Finals.

In 2023, Parker signed with the Las Vegas Aces. Parker hurt her foot during the season. But the Aces won the Finals!

2021 WNBA FINALS

TIMELINE

— 2004 —

Parker wins the slam dunk contest at the McDonald's All American Game

— 2008 —

Parker is drafted by the Sparks

— 2012 —

Parker helps Team USA win gold at the London Summer Olympics

— 2016 —
Parker wins her first WNBA Finals with the Sparks

— 2021 —
Parker helps the Sky win the Finals

PARKER'S FUTURE

Parker started a podcast in 2021. In 2023, she was the first woman to be a game analyst for the NBA All-Star Game. She also works with groups that help lower the cost of youth sports.

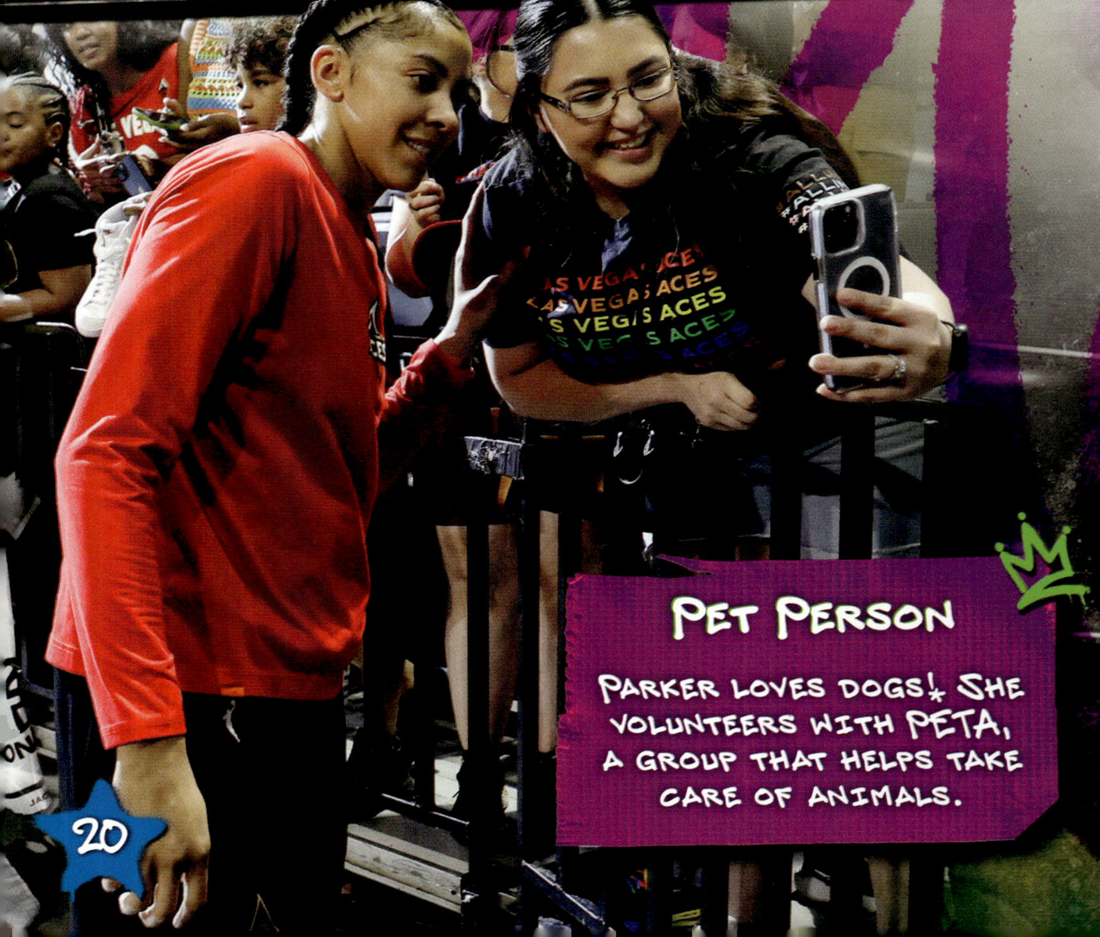

PET PERSON

PARKER LOVES DOGS! SHE VOLUNTEERS WITH PETA, A GROUP THAT HELPS TAKE CARE OF ANIMALS.

In 2024, Parker decided to stop playing in the WNBA. But she plans to stay close to the sport as a game analyst!

GLOSSARY

All-Star Game—a game between the best players in a league

center—a player in basketball who often blocks shots and gets rebounds

championships—contests to decide the best team or person

defensive—related to a group of players who try to stop the opposing team from scoring

drafted—chose by a process where professional teams choose high school and college athletes to play for them

Finals—the championship series of the Women's National Basketball Association

forward—a basketball player who plays close to the net

game analyst—a person who talks about the game and describes the players

most valuable player—the best player in a year, game, or series; the most valuable player is often called the MVP.

Olympic—related to the Olympic Games; the Olympic Games are worldwide summer or winter sports contests held in a different country every four years.

rookie—a first-year player in a sports league

semifinals—the series of games played to determine which teams play in the final series of a sports tournament

slam dunks—shots in which a player pushes the basketball forcefully down through the basket

Women's National Basketball Association—a league for professional basketball in the United States; the Women's National Basketball Association is often called the WNBA.

TO LEARN MORE

AT THE LIBRARY

Rule, Heather. *Candace Parker.* Lake Elmo, Minn.: Focus Readers, 2022.

Sabelko, Rebecca. *Diana Taurasi.* Minneapolis, Minn.: Bellwether Media, 2023.

Whiting, Jim. *The Story of the Los Angeles Sparks.* Mankato, Minn.: Creative Education, 2024.

ON THE WEB

FACTSURFER

Factsurfer.com gives you a safe, fun way to find more information.

1. Go to www.factsurfer.com
2. Enter "Candace Parker" into the search box and click 🔍.
3. Select your book cover to see a list of related content.

INDEX

The images in this book are reproduced through the courtesy of: Erica Denhoff/ Icon Sportswire/ AP Images, cover; Ethan Miller/ Staff/ Getty Images, pp. 3, 19, 20; Christian Petersen/ Staff/ Getty Images, pp. 4, 5, 14; Rich von Biberstein/ Icon Sportswire/ AP Images, p. 6; Lindsey Wasson/ AP Images, p. 7 (Candace Parker), 23; Jim McIsaac/ Staff/ Getty, p. 8; Sea Cow/ Wikipedia, p. 9; Icon Sports Wire/ Contributor/ Getty Images, p. 10; Al Messerschmidt/ Stringer/ Getty Images, p. 11 (2008 NCAA Women's Final Four Championship); grey_and, p. 11 (soccer); MacMontree, p. 11 (almonds); Banana Images, p. 11 (gingerbread latte); Triff, p. 11 (history); Jeff Gross/ Staff/ Getty Images, p. 12; Miami Herald/ Contributor, p. 13; Cal Sport Media/ Alamy, p. 15 (All-Star Game); 4kclips, p. 15 (Los Angeles Sparks stadium); Serhii Chrucky/ Alamy; p. 15 (Chicago Sky stadium); JHVEPhoto, p. 15 (Las Vegas Aces stadium); Hannah Foslien/ Stringer/ Getty Images, pp. 16, 19 (2016); Douglas P. DeFelice/ Contributor/ Getty, p. 17; SPP Sport Press Photo./ Alamy, p. 18 (Candace Parker); Los Angeles Sparks/ Wikipedia, p. 18 (2008); Tony Baggett, p. 18 (2012); Stacy Revere/ Staff, p. 19 (2021); Kelly Balch/ Stringer/ Getty Images, p. 21.